Could it be?
A tough Teddie?

Tough
Teddies

D1529551

ALSO BY SIMON BOND

101 Uses for a Dead Cat

101 More Uses for a Dead Cat

Unspeakable Acts

Bizarre Sights and Odd Visions

Tough Teddies

and other bears

by Simon Bond

Clarkson N. Potter, Inc./Publishers
DISTRIBUTED BY CROWN PUBLISHERS, INC. NEW YORK

For Linda

Published by Clarkson N. Potter, Inc., One Park Avenue, New York,
New York 10016

CLARKSON N. POTTER, POTTER, and colophon are trademarks of
Clarkson N. Potter, Inc.

Manufactured in the United States of America

Library of Congress Cataloging in Publication Data

Bond, Simon.
    Tough teddies and other bears.

      1. Teddy bears—Caricatures and cartoons.
2. American wit and humor, Pictorial.   I. Title.

NC1429.B663A4   1985   741.5'973   85-3518
ISBN 0-517-55832-7

10 9 8 7 6 5 4 3 2 1

First Edition

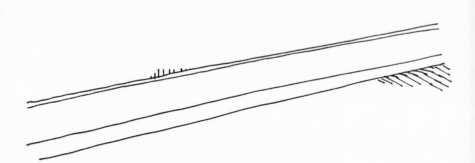

"One medium rare and one with honey."

INSECURITY HITS WALL STREET

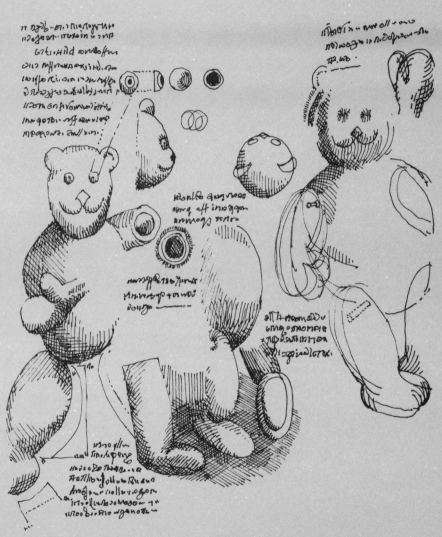

Leonardo's First Drawings

Picasso's teddy

1910

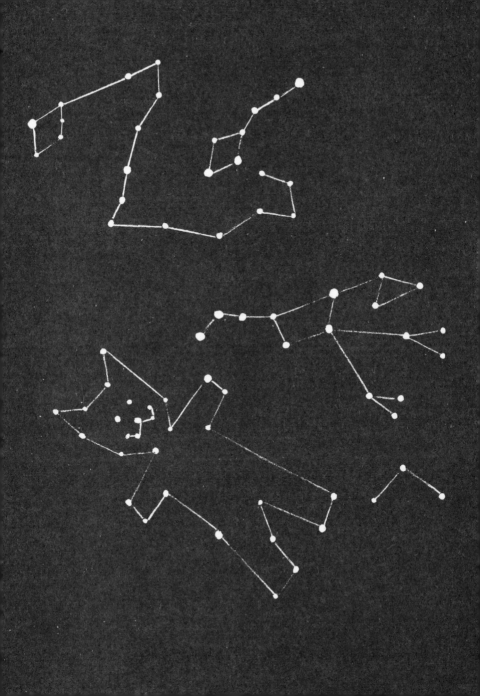

"If he can do that, I reckon he's got what it takes."

HOTEL
HEARTLESS

BATHROC

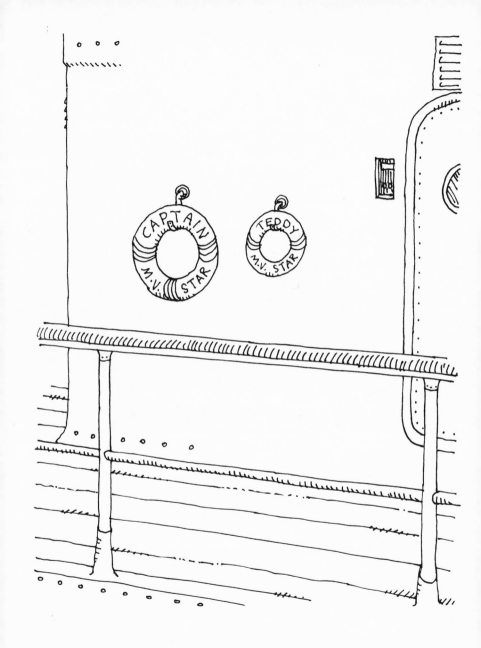

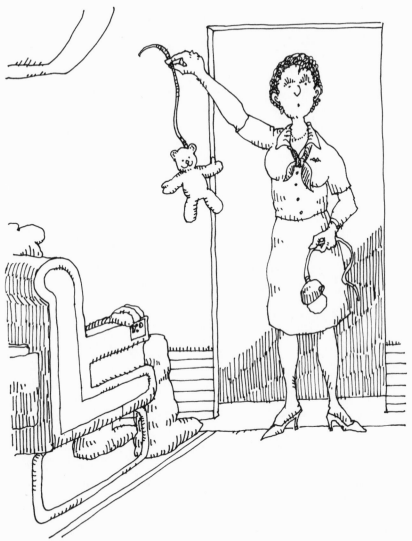

"... and in the case of continuing emergency, a teddy will drop into your lap from the compartment above."

" So you'd better start talking or the teddy takes a dive...."

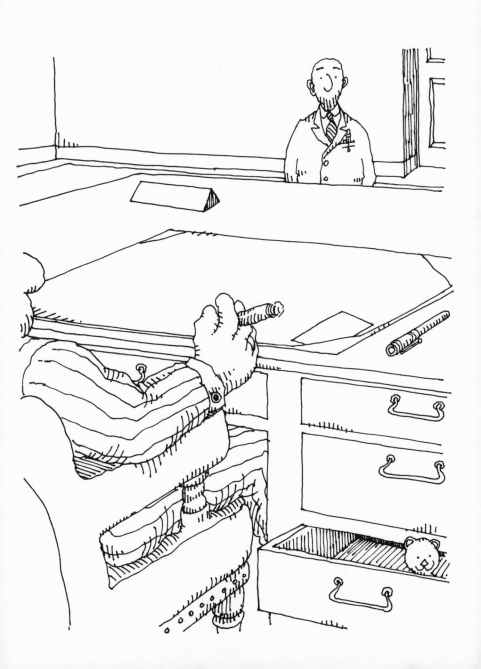

"Welcome and here are your ear and arm back."

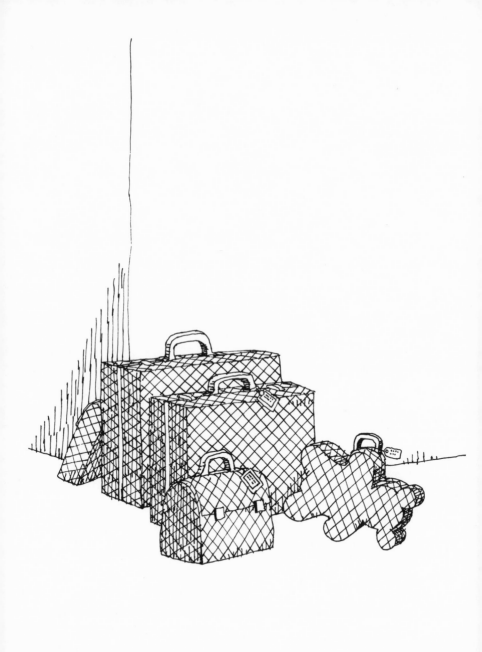

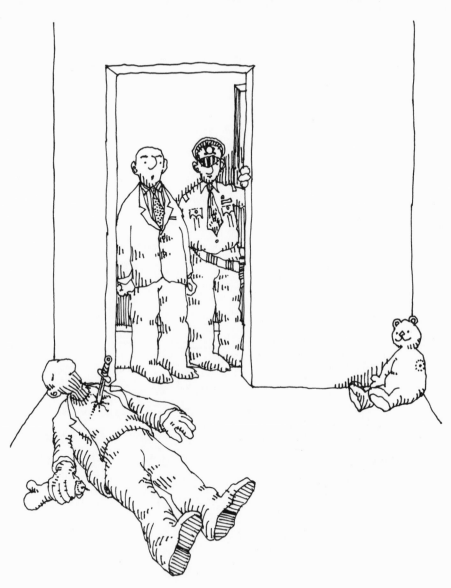

"I think we can put this one down as self-defense, Mulligan."

"...and please stop the little bastard chewing my ears."

STUPIDITY No 1

TEDDY BEARS
IN CAPTIVITY

TEDDY BEARS IN THE WILD

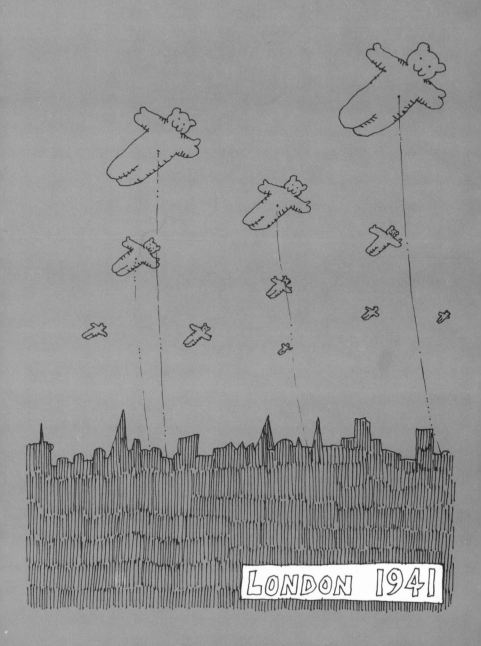

LONDON 1941

IN CASE OF
ANXIETY
BREAK GLASS

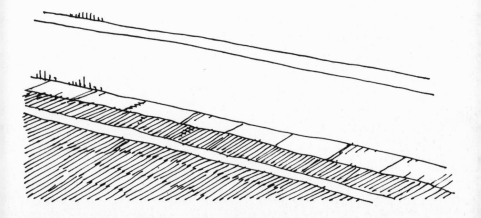

ROMULUS & REMUS
(AND THEIR BROTHER DEREK)

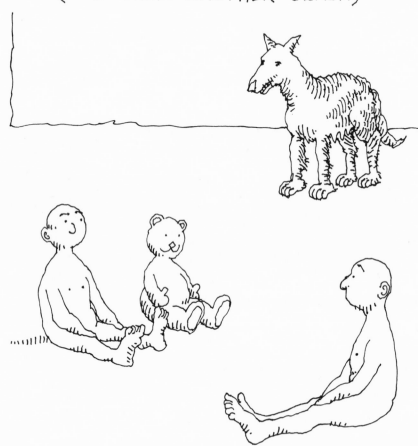

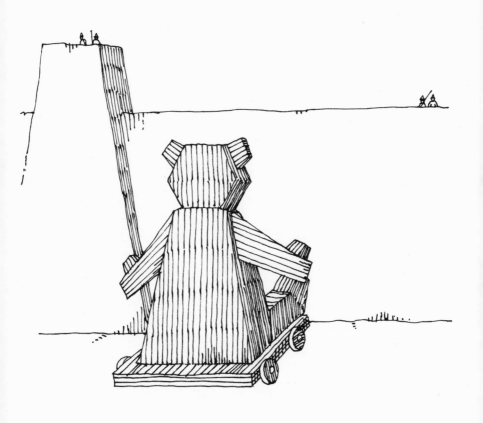

THE FIRST ATTEMPT

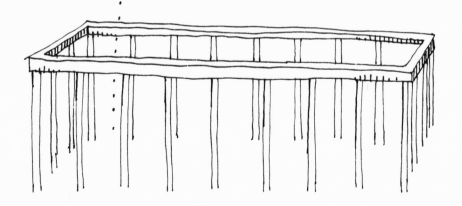

WERNHER VON BRAUN'S
FIRST EXPERIMENT

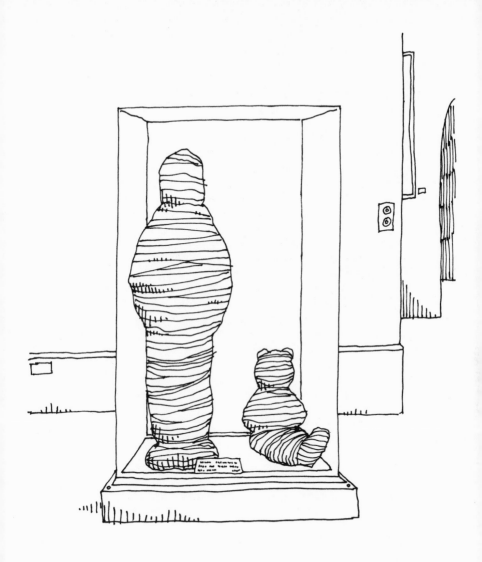

"You'll find them a very friendly tribe."

THE TEDDY TEST

①

②

③

④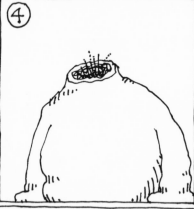

○ LORD NELSON   ○ VINCENT VAN GOGH
○ CHARLES MANSON   ○ RICHARD III

Match each Teddy with its very famous owner.

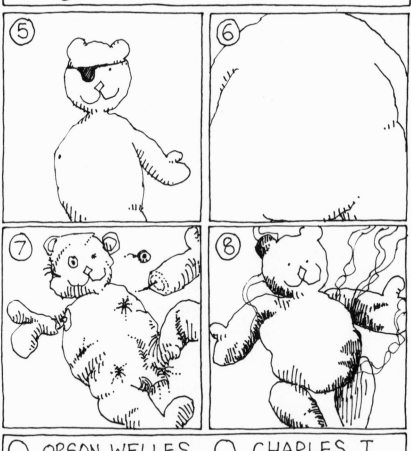

⑤

⑥

⑦

⑧

○ ORSON WELLES   ○ CHARLES I
○ JOAN OF ARC   ○ CYRANO DE BERGERAC

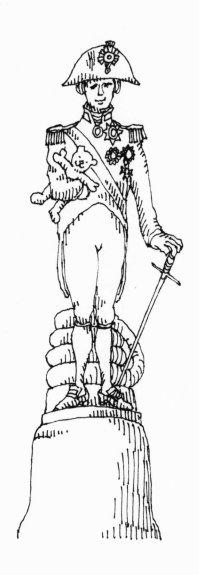

THE
3 BEARS

THE POCKET
VERSION

THE
END OF
INNOCENCE...

...but in the end love conquers all.

About the Author

SIMON BOND has always liked anything smaller than
himself and, accordingly, is the proud owner of five
teddy bears. He is hoping to acquire more in the future
through either marriage or theft.